Presidential
Medal of Freedom
Winners

Collective Biographies

Presidential Medal of Freedom Winners

Carmen Bredeson

Enslow Publishers, Inc.

44 Fadem Road	PO Box 38
Box 699	Aldershot
Springfield, NJ 07081	Hants GU12 6BP
USA	UK

Library of Congress Cataloging-in-Publication Data

Bredeson, Carmen.
    Presidential Medal of Freedom winners / Carmen Bredeson.
       p. cm. — (Collective biographies)
    Includes bibliographical references and index.
    Contents: Helen Keller—Marian Anderson—Margaret Chase
Smith—Margaret Mead—Ralph Bunche—Joe DiMaggio—Hector
Garcia—Cesar Chavez—Neil Armstrong—Colin Powell.
    ISBN 0-89490-705-0
    1. United States—Biography—Juvenile literature. 2. Presidential Medal of
Freedom—Juvenile literature. [1. United States—Biography. 2. Presidential
Medal of Freedom.] I. Title. II. Series.
CT214.B65 1996
973'.099—dc20
[B]   96-1743
                                                       CIP
                                                       AC

Printed in the United States of America

10 9 8 7 6 5 4 3 2 1

Illustration Credits:
AP/Wide World Photos, p. 54; Courtesy of Hector Garcia, pp. 56, 62;
Department of Defense, pp. 82, 89; Library of Congress, p. 24; National
Archives, pp. 8, 14, 16, 21, 29, 32, 38, 40, 46, 48, 72, 80; The Institute of
Texan Cultures, the *San Antonio Light* Collection, pp. 64, 70.

Cover Illustration:
Courtesy of Colin Powell

Contents

Preface

In a 1990 interview, Colin Powell said: "People keep asking what is the secret to my success. There isn't any secret. I work hard. I spend long hours. I don't get distracted from the task before me."[1]

Each of the Presidential Medal of Freedom recipients in this book worked extremely hard to achieve success. Even though Helen Keller was both blind and deaf, she graduated from college, wrote books, and helped improve the lives of other physically challenged people. Hector Garcia and Cesar Chavez also spent countless hours making life better for the poor Hispanic Americans that they knew.

Marian Anderson's African-American heritage appeared to be a barrier at the beginning of her career. Instead of giving up in the face of difficulty, the gifted singer overcame the obstacles in her path and excelled in her profession. Her wonderful voice entertained and inspired many who heard her sing. Joe DiMaggio's skill on the baseball field also brought joy to thousands of Americans as they watched the "Yankee Clipper" slam ball after ball into the air.

Who can forget the pictures of the first steps that Neil Armstrong took on the surface of the Moon in 1969? He helped bring the mysteries of space into our own living rooms. Colin Powell also became a familiar figure on our television screens during the Persian Gulf War in 1991. His informative news conferences helped us understand the complexities of that time.

More than three hundred people have been awarded the Presidential Medal of Freedom. It was first established by President Harry Truman in 1945 and was originally called the Medal of Freedom. It was the nation's highest civilian award, and Truman presented it to those who had performed meritorious acts or services during World War II.

In 1963, President John F. Kennedy reestablished the award and named it the Presidential Medal of Freedom. It would be presented to any American or foreigner, military or nonmilitary, who made a significant contribution to life in the United States. Some medals were awarded to those who helped protect our national security and promote world peace. Other medals were given to people who used their talents to create new businesses and products so that our lives would be easier. Some Presidential Medal of Freedom recipients enhanced our cultural lives with their acting, singing, or athletic abilities.

The people in this book represent only a small number of those who have been awarded the Presidential Medal of Freedom. These ten were chosen because they made a significant impact on some area of life in the United States. Each of their contributions is different from the others, but each is unique and valuable in its own way.

Helen Keller

Helen Keller
(1880–1968)

"Then, in the dreary month of February, came the illness which closed my eyes and ears and plunged me into the unconsciousness of a new-born baby."[1] Life would never be the same for Helen Keller. The curious and friendly toddler was suddenly shut off from the sounds and sights around her. No longer would she hear her mother's voice or see the flowers that bloomed around the Keller's small house in Tuscumbia, Alabama. Her world would be forever dark and silent.

Helen was born on June 27, 1880, to Arthur and Kate Keller. During her first eighteen months, she was an energetic and happy child. Then came the terrible illness and fever that raged for days. Even though the doctor said that Helen would not live, she managed to survive. Her family rejoiced as the fever left the child's small body. It soon became apparent, however, that something was wrong.

The cheerful, curious child that the Kellers had known was suddenly frightened, withdrawn, and unable to communicate with those around her. In a short time, the Kellers knew that their little daughter could no longer see or hear. Helen's familiar world had been taken from her, and she spent hours huddled in her mother's lap.

As some of her fear receded, Helen began to explore her surroundings and gradually learned to feel her way around the house and yard. She occasionally could make her wishes known by using simple signs. More often though, Helen was not understood, and she screamed and cried in frustration. As she grew older, her outbursts became more frequent.

In an effort to find someone to help Helen, the Kellers consulted with the Perkins Institution for the Blind located in Boston, Massachusetts. Arrangements were made for a teacher to come and live with the Kellers. Twenty-year-old Anne Mansfield Sullivan was chosen for the job. Sullivan had also been blind as a child, but an operation during her teen years had given her limited vision. Helen Keller said that the arrival of Anne Sullivan on March 3, 1887, was the most important day in her life.[2]

On that day, six-year-old Helen was sitting on the front porch when she felt the footsteps of someone approaching. Thinking that it was her mother, she stretched out her hand. "Some one took it, and I was caught up and held close in the arms of her who had come to reveal all things to me, and, more than all things else, to love me."[3]

In her work with the blind, Anne Sullivan used a method called the manual alphabet to communicate with her students. Sullivan held the fingers of one hand in a different position for each letter of the alphabet. Her student lightly placed a hand over Sullivan's fingers to "read" the signals that were being sent. Each word had to be spelled out letter by letter.

On the morning after Sullivan's arrival, she began to try to teach Helen the manual alphabet. She gave a doll to Helen and then spelled d-o-l-l into her hand, over and over. As the pair made their way around the house, Sullivan spelled the names of other objects into Helen's hand. The child did not yet understand the connection between the objects and the finger movements, but she began to imitate the motions that her teacher made.

Four weeks after Anne Sullivan arrived in Alabama, she and Helen were walking in the garden. Someone was getting water from the well, and Sullivan placed one of Helen's hands under the flowing water. Into the child's other hand, she spelled w-a-t-e-r over and over. Helen Keller later wrote:

> I stood still, my whole attention fixed upon the motions of her fingers. Suddenly, I felt a misty consciousness as of something forgotten — a thrill of returning thought; and somehow the mystery of language was revealed to me. I

knew then that "w-a-t-e-r" meant the wonderful cool something that was flowing over my hand. That living word awakened my soul, gave it light, hope, joy, set it free![4]

Gradually, over the next few months, Helen learned how to spell the names of the things in her world and once again to communicate with those around her. As her confidence grew, Helen's tantrums stopped and were replaced by an eagerness to learn.

After three years with Anne Sullivan, Helen Keller knew the manual alphabet and had also learned to read Braille. The Braille alphabet consists of patterns of small, raised dots that represent each of the letters in the alphabet. Using both of the methods, Helen learned to read and write. Helen was not satisfied with only knowing how to communicate with her hands though. She wanted to learn to speak.

In 1890, Sarah Fuller, the principal of a nearby school, agreed to try to teach Helen to speak. She had Helen lightly touch her lips and tongue to feel their positions when a sound was made. Gradually Helen learned to make those same motions with her mouth and began to make sounds. In the beginning, her words were almost impossible to understand. With constant coaching from Anne Sullivan and Sarah Fuller, Helen eventually learned to speak more clearly. With a great deal of practice, she also mastered the art of reading lips with her fingers.

After years of hard work, Helen Keller was able to communicate with everyone she met by reading their lips with her fingers. She nearly stopped using the manual alphabet. It was not discarded, though, because she still needed it in the classroom. In order for her to attend regular classes, Sullivan had to be there next to her, spelling all of the teacher's comments into her hand.

Some of Helen's textbooks were translated into Braille so she could read them herself. The others were read aloud by Anne Sullivan while her student lipread the words. Much of Helen's homework was completed on a typewriter and then checked by Sullivan. Helen successfully finished high school in 1900 and was admitted to Radcliffe College in Cambridge, Massachusetts, that same year.

It took a great deal of time and effort for Helen Keller to complete her assignments, always with the constant assistance of Anne Sullivan. In addition to her difficult courses, Keller worked on her autobiography with Harvard University literature professor John Macy. *The Story of My Life,* published in 1903, detailed Keller's childhood and life after she started to attend school.

During Keller's graduation from Radcliffe College in 1904, she was given a standing ovation by her fellow students. She was disappointed that Anne Sullivan was not also recognized for her role in Keller's education.[5] She later said about Sullivan: "All the best of me belongs to her—there is not a talent, or an inspiration or a joy in me that has not been awakened by her loving touch."[6]

In school, Helen Keller (left) relied on the constant assistance of Anne Sullivan (right).

After college, Anne Sullivan and Helen Keller moved to Wrentham, Massachusetts. In 1905, Anne Sullivan and John Macy were married, but only after he agreed that Helen Keller could remain with them. Keller continued to write, and in 1908, *The World I Live In* was published, followed by *Out of the Dark* in 1913. In 1914, the marriage of John Macy and Anne Sullivan ended. A young woman named Polly Thompson moved in with Keller and Sullivan and became their secretary.

In 1924, Helen Keller became involved with the newly formed American Foundation for the Blind. She began to raise funds for the organization and made many lecture tours to inform others of the difficulties the blind faced.

When asked about her life, Helen Keller once said: "My life has been happy because I have had wonderful friends and plenty of interesting work to do. I seldom think about my limitations, and they never make me sad."[7] In 1960, a play called *The Miracle Worker* was written about Keller's life. It was later made into a movie of the same name.

In 1964, eighty-four-year-old Helen Keller was invited to Washington, D.C. In a ceremony at the White House, President Lyndon Johnson awarded Keller the Presidential Medal of Freedom. Helen Keller died on June 1, 1968.

Marian Anderson

Marian Anderson
(1897–1993)

On a crisp, clear Easter morning in 1939, people began to gather in front of the Lincoln Memorial in Washington, D.C. By 4 P.M., a crowd of seventy-five thousand lined the sides of the Reflecting Pool that shimmered in front of the enormous statue of Abraham Lincoln. At 4:30 P.M., Marian Anderson stepped out of a car and made her way to the steps of the monument amid the cheers of those gathered before her. Dressed in a long velvet gown and a fur coat, the stately Anderson closed her eyes and began to sing "America."

Song after song followed, including Schubert's "Ave Maria" and several spirituals. When she repeatedly tried to end the concert, the crowd went wild with applause and would not let her leave. Marian Anderson said to her admiring fans: "The immensity of this affair has done so much to me, I'm not up to giving a nice speech. I thank you from the bottom of my heart, again and again."[1]

Marian Anderson was born on February 17, 1897, to John and Annie Anderson in South Philadelphia, Pennsylvania. The Andersons were also the parents of two other daughters, Alyce and Ethel. Marian first sang in the children's choir of the Union Baptist Church at age six but moved to the adult choir when she was eight. Even at that early age, Marian had a mature and rich voice. Marian Anderson's father died when she was ten, and the young girl helped support her family by singing at church concerts.

Even though there was not enough money for Marian to have music lessons, her remarkable voice continued to improve. During her second year at South Philadelphia High School, her singing attracted the attention of John Thomas Butler, an African-American actor. He arranged a visit between Marian and Mary Patterson, a voice coach in Philadelphia. After hearing Marian sing, Patterson agreed to teach the girl for free. Later the Philadelphia Choral Society raised money to pay for Marian's voice lessons with Agnes Reifsnyder, a well-known voice teacher in the area.

When Anderson was nineteen, she auditioned with Giuseppe Boghetti, a world renowned voice teacher. He later said that when he heard the tall, calm girl sing for the first time, it brought tears to his eyes.[2] Through Boghetti, Anderson's name was entered in a singing contest with three hundred other participants. She won the competition and was given the opportunity to sing at Lewisohn Stadium in New York, accompanied by the New York Philharmonic Orchestra. In spite of her success at the concert, there were few additional requests for her to sing. Many said: "A wonderful voice—it's too bad that she's a Negro."[3]

Marian Anderson left the United States in 1929 to study and perform in Europe. During the next few years, she appeared before hundreds of audiences and attracted many fans. She sang for King Christian in Copenhagen, Denmark, and for King Gustav in Stockholm, Sweden. In one year alone, Anderson gave more than one hundred concerts. In 1935, Marian Anderson returned to the United States for a recital at New York's Town Hall. The performance was a huge success, and Anderson was hailed as a "new high priestess of song."[4]

In 1939, Anderson's agent tried to arrange a concert in Constitution Hall, located in Washington, D.C. The owners of the hall, the Daughters of the American Revolution (DAR), denied permission for Anderson to perform there because she was an African American. (The DAR is an organization whose members are direct descendants of soldiers or patriots of the American Revolution.) Fans and fellow musicians loudly protested the DAR's decision. Marian Anderson said, "I am shocked beyond words to be barred from the capital of my country after having appeared in almost every other capital in the world."[5]

As a result of the DAR's decision, First Lady Eleanor Roosevelt resigned her membership in the organization and arranged the now-famous Lincoln Memorial concert for Anderson. On that memorable April day in 1939, Harold Ickes, secretary of the interior, introduced Marian Anderson to the crowd and said, ". . . in this great auditorium under the sky, all of us are free."[6] Anderson later said about the concert, "I could see that my significance as an individual was small in this affair. I had become, whether I like it or not, a symbol, representing my people. I had to appear."[7]

After the Lincoln Memorial appearance, Marian Anderson became one of the most popular and successful performers in America. Her repertoire was made up of more than two hundred songs in nine languages. When asked how she learned so many new songs, Anderson replied, "Each singer has his own way of learning a song. I like to hear the melody first, to get something from the music before I have begun serious work on the words."[8] Marian Anderson's performances often included a selection of spirituals. She said, "I do not have to tell you that I dearly love the Negro spirituals. They are the unburdenings of the sorrows of an entire race."[9]

In spite of her immense popularity, Marian Anderson often had to carry her own luggage and

First Lady Eleanor Roosevelt resigned her DAR membership as a show of support for her friend Marian Anderson.

enter hotels and concert halls through back doors. That was common treatment for many African Americans in the United States prior to the civil rights movement of the 1950s and 1960s. A newspaper article about Marian Anderson said:

> The handicaps which she had to overcome in order to attain her present position in the world of music have left no apparent hard feeling. Past slurs and indignities have been forgotten, and she rises above all prejudices, regarding them as the result of ignorance rather than of hatred.[10]

In 1943 Marian Anderson and architect Orpheus Fisher were married. In 1955, Anderson published her autobiography, *My Lord, What a Morning.* During that same year, she became the first African American to perform at the Metropolitan Opera House in New York City. She sang the role of Ulrica in "The Masquerade Ball" by Giuseppi Verdi.

Two years after Anderson's operatic debut at the Met, President Dwight Eisenhower invited her to sing at his 1957 inaugural ball. President John Kennedy also requested a performance by Anderson at his inaugural ball in 1961. In a White House ceremony in 1963, President Lyndon Johnson presented the Presidential Medal of Freedom to Marian Anderson. President John Kennedy selected Anderson for the honor, but he was assassinated before he could present the award.

In 1965, sixty-eight-year-old Marian Anderson began a final, nationwide tour with a concert at Constitution Hall. She had been denied permission to perform in that same hall in 1939. After the months-long tour, Anderson sang before an audience of twenty-nine hundred at Carnegie Hall. She then announced her retirement and said, "This farewell is not the end of anything. We are not out of the civil-rights struggle, we do not rule out marches in the future, we do not intend to sit and twiddle our thumbs."[11]

After her farewell concert, Marian Anderson retired to the home in New England that she shared with her husband of twenty-two years, Orpheus Fisher. In a 1991 documentary for public television, Anderson said, "I hadn't set out to change the world in any way. Whatever I am, it is a culmination of the goodwill of people who, regardless of anything else, saw me as I am, and not as somebody else."[12]

At the age of ninety-three, Marian Anderson was interviewed in her Connecticut farmhouse. Looking back at her life, Anderson said, "It is my honest belief that to contribute to the betterment of something, one can do it best in the medium through which one expresses one's self most easily."[13] Song was Marian Anderson's medium.

The famous Italian conductor Arturo Toscannini once said to Anderson, "Yours is a voice such as one hears once in a hundred years."[14] Marian Anderson died in 1993 at the age of ninety-six.

Margaret Chase Smith

Margaret Chase Smith
(1897–1995)

When Margaret Chase Smith was well into her ninth decade, she said, "I have great energy because I love life. I ignore my age."[1] In her long life, Smith accomplished many things. She was the first woman to be elected to both the United States House of Representatives and the Senate. She was also the first woman to seek the nomination for President by a major political party. Her list of accomplishments span a political career of more than thirty years.

Life began for Margaret Chase in Skowhegan, Maine, on December 14, 1897. Her father, George Chase, was a barber, and her mother, Carrie Murray Chase, was a part-time waitress. Margaret grew up the oldest of six children in a small house next door to the barber shop. The family enjoyed weekend fishing trips and other outdoor activities.

When Margaret was just twelve years old, she got a job stocking the shelves at a local store for ten cents an hour. During high school, Margaret worked part-time as a telephone operator. She graduated from Skowhegan High School in 1916 but could not afford to go to college. After her graduation, Margaret Chase taught in a one-room schoolhouse for seven months. (In 1916, a college degree was not necessary to become a teacher.) After her time in the classroom, Chase returned to the local telephone company.

In 1919, Margaret Chase was hired by the local newspaper, *The Independent Reporter,* where she served as the circulation manager. It was there that she met her future husband, Clyde H. Smith, co-owner of the paper and twenty-one years older than Chase. After a courtship that lasted several years, the couple married on May 14, 1930.

Clyde Smith, a Skowhegan businessman, was active in both local and state politics. In 1936, he was elected to the United States House of Representatives. During Clyde Smith's years as a representative, Margaret Chase Smith worked as his aide. The long work days provided her with a first-hand look at the world of government.

In 1940, Clyde Smith planned to run for reelection to the House. Just before the filing deadline for the primary elections, he suffered a heart attack and had to withdraw his name. Before his death on April 8, 1940, Smith urged his wife to run for the congressional seat in his place. Margaret Chase Smith was elected to the seventy-seventh Congress of the United States. After the intensive campaign, she said, "I'd been taught by my husband not to do it halfway."[2]

Margaret Chase Smith's first term in Congress passed quickly, and she was reelected by the voters of Maine in 1942, 1944, and 1946. In 1943, she was appointed to the Naval Affairs Committee. As part of that committee, she embarked on a twenty-five-thousand-mile tour to inspect United States military bases in the South Pacific. The fact-finding mission led to her efforts to improve the status of women who served in Naval auxiliary units during World War II.

In 1947, during Margaret Chase Smith's fourth term in the House, Maine Senator Wallace White announced that he would not run again. Smith, a Republican, decided to run for the Senate seat and entered the primary race. She amassed more votes than the combined totals of the three other Republican contenders. With the general election before her, Margaret Smith began to campaign.

Margaret Chase Smith's campaign for the Senate was conducted with very limited funds. Instead of spending money on expensive advertising, Smith visited more than six hundred communities in Maine and personally met many of the state's residents. Her hard work paid off with the defeat of her Democratic opponent in the general election on September 18, 1948.

During Smith's freshman term in the Senate, the controversial agenda set forth by Republican Senator Joseph McCarthy of Wisconsin was the subject of much discussion. McCarthy accused a variety of public figures of belonging to the Communist party. Even though he had no proof to support his accusations, his verbal attacks continued to escalate.

On June 1, 1950, Senator Margaret Chase Smith appeared before the United States Senate and delivered her first major speech, which she called "A Declaration of Conscience." Even though she did not refer to Senator McCarthy by name, the audience was aware of the object of her remarks. Smith denounced McCarthy for fostering an atmosphere of hate and suspicion. She said that the Republican party should not support an agenda that was based on ". . . fear, ignorance, bigotry, and smear."[3]

Margaret Chase Smith received a great deal of publicity for her statements against McCarthy. After the speech, McCarthy referred to Smith and the six other Republican senators who signed her declaration as "Snow White and the Six Dwarfs."[4] McCarthy continued his verbal attacks for several more years until a special investigation found that his claims were unsubstantiated. Joseph McCarthy was censured by the Senate in 1954. Margaret Chase Smith's speech in 1950 was the first public outcry in protest of McCarthy's underhanded tactics.

Margaret Chase Smith received a great deal of publicity for her statements against Senator Joseph McCarthy. Here, she enjoys some time in her garden.

When asked about her career in politics, Smith replied, "The Senate is my whole life. I have no family, no time-consuming hobbies. I have only myself and my job as United States Senator."[5] By 1964, Margaret Chase Smith was a member of the Armed Services and Appropriations Committees as well as the ranking Republican on the Aeronautical and Space Sciences Committee. As the 1964 elections approached, Smith was faced with a tough decision. Would she throw her hat into the ring and become a candidate for President? Senator Smith revealed her answer on January 27, 1964. In spite of the fact that no woman had ever before been nominated for President by a major political party, Smith decided to enter the campaign.

At the time of her announcement, Smith outranked most of the members of the United States Senate in terms of seniority. In addition, she had been present at more than fifteen hundred consecutive roll-call votes, setting a record for attendance. After her announcement, Smith said, "Whether or not there is a future in politics for women depends upon the women themselves." She continued, "The inescapable fact is that they hold the control of the public offices with their majority voting power."[6]

A 1963 census report showed that there were nearly 58 million women age twenty-one and over living in the United States. That compared to just over 54 million men in the same age group.[7] In spite of the fact that there were potentially nearly 4 million more female than male voters, Margaret Chase Smith did not win the Republican nomination for President in 1964. That spot on the ticket went to Senator Barry Goldwater, who was ultimately defeated by President Lyndon Johnson.

Nationally, women were not granted the right to vote until 1920. It had taken nearly one hundred years of protests before women were able to be heard at the ballot box. Their presence in Congress had also been slow to materialize. In 1949, there was one woman in the United States Senate and nine women in the House of Representatives. By 1993, the number had risen to seven women in the Senate and forty-seven in the House, or about 10 percent of the total members of Congress.[8]

Margaret Chase Smith's tenure in Congress was a long and distinguished one that finally ended with her failure to win a fifth term in the Senate in 1974. Seventy-six-year-old Senator Smith was defeated by her Democratic opponent, William Hathaway. After her defeat, Margaret Chase Smith returned to Skowhegan, Maine.

In 1989, ninety-two-year-old Margaret Chase Smith was awarded the Presidential Medal of Freedom by President George Bush. Smith continued to be active and alert until her death at age ninety-seven on May 29, 1995. After her death, former President Bush said: "Margaret Chase set a wonderful example of public service for all Americans."[9]

Margaret Mead

Margaret Mead

(1901–1978)

Even as a child, Margaret Mead observed people and their behavior. Her mother, Emily Fogg Mead, was a sociologist. Margaret's father, Edward Mead, was a professor of economics at the University of Pennsylvania. As a part of his job, Professor Mead traveled around the state and helped establish new branches of the university. His work required the family to move often. Margaret had many opportunities to meet new people and adjust to new situations.

When she was just six years old, the Mead family attended an Italian-American wedding. After they returned home, Margaret reported her observations about the ceremony to her mother, who was writing a book about immigrants. In addition, Margaret was encouraged by her grandmother to take notes on the behavior of her younger brother and two sisters.

Born in Philadelphia, Pennsylvania, on December 16, 1901, Margaret Mead's elementary school years were spent mostly at home. She was tutored by her grandmother, Martha Mead, who was a former teacher. When Margaret was a little older, she attended junior and senior high school for six years.

After her high school graduation in 1919, Margaret Mead enrolled at her father's alma mater, DePauw University, located in Greencastle, Indiana. She remained there only one year, then transferred to Barnard College in New York City. During her senior year, Mead took a class taught by Franz Boas. The well-known professor taught anthropology, which is the study of the origins, customs, and beliefs of human beings. After the completion of Boas's class, Mead decided to study anthropology in graduate school.

In 1923, Margaret Mead graduated from Barnard College with a degree in psychology. Shortly after her graduation, Mead married Luther Cressman, the first of her three husbands. The young couple moved into an apartment in New York City, where Cressman was a minister and student. Mead enrolled in a graduate program in anthropology at Columbia University. As part of her graduate studies, Mead was required to complete a field study. She decided to travel to the South Pacific to a group of Polynesian islands that are called American Samoa. She wanted to observe teenage girls who lived on the islands to discover if they experienced the same kinds of problems during puberty that many American girls have.

On August 31, 1925, twenty-three-year-old Margaret Mead arrived on the island of Tutuila. She moved into a hotel in the port city of Pago Pago for several weeks and had a crash course in the Samoan language. When she had learned enough Samoan to be able to communicate, Mead went to a nearby village where arrangements had been made for her to stay in the chief's house. During her time with the chief's family, Mead learned some of the customs of the people. She ate Samoan food, danced at their festivals, and drank kava, a ceremonial beverage.

After several weeks in the village, Mead returned to Pago Pago, where she met Ruth Holt, an American who lived on the island of Tau. Holt's home was within walking distance of three Samoan villages, and Holt and her husband invited Mead to live with them while she conducted additional studies. Mead accompanied Ruth Holt to Tau, which was located one hundred miles from the island of Tutuila.

On the island of Tau, Mead selected fifty girls to observe who lived in three different villages. She spent her days with various groups of the girls. She listened as they talked about themselves, and she watched their behavior. Mead later wrote: "Every word, grunt, scratch, stomachache, change of wearing apparel, snatch of song sung on the road or just flung over someone else's wall is *relevant.*"[1] When she returned to Ruth Holt's home in the evening, Mead recorded her observations.

Margaret Mead discovered that adolescence among the Samoan girls was not an especially difficult time. Life in the villages was less competitive than life in the United States. In addition, attitudes concerning teenage sexuality were more open and permissive, thereby creating less conflict in the lives of the girls. Mead's observations about the Samoan girls would evolve into a book called *Coming of Age in Samoa.* The best-seller was published in 1928, the same year that the divorced Mead married fellow anthropologist Reo Fortune.

Margaret Mead said about *Coming of Age in Samoa:*

> I did not write it as a popular book, but only with the hope that it would be intelligible to those who might make the best use of its theme, that adolescence need not be the time of stress and strain which Western society makes it . . .[2]

Margaret Mead's study in Samoa was just the first in a long career of field studies. During the years 1928 to 1933, she observed the children of four tribes in New Guinea and learned seven different native languages. *Growing Up in New Guinea* was published in 1930. About her interest in primitive societies, Mead wrote:

> Even in remote parts of the world ways of life about which nothing was known were

vanishing before the onslaught of modern civilization. The work of recording these unknown ways of life had to be done now—*now*—or they would be lost forever.[3]

After Mead's marriage to Reo Fortune ended in divorce, she married biologist Gregory Bateson in 1936. A daughter, Mary Catherine, was born to the couple in 1939. When Margaret Mead was not in some remote location, she served for more than forty years as a curator at the American Museum of Natural History in New York City. Mead's attention was not directed just to primitive culture. She wrote and spoke about a variety of subjects that included topics from pollution to day care to drugs. Her 1970 book, *Culture and Commitment,* examined problems that American young people of the 1960s experienced. *A Way of Seeing,* also published in 1970, contained Mead's views about war, the environment, and overpopulation.

Margaret Mead's energy seemed boundless, even into her later years. Up at 5 A.M. to teach a class or catch a plane, she often wore a cape and carried a long, forked stick. Early in her career, Mead broke her ankle, and it remained weak for the rest of her life. Instead of using an ordinary cane, she chose a shoulder-high stick made of cherry wood to help her walk.

Mead had many followers who admired her work and her stamina. In December 1976, the American Museum of Natural History took out a

Margaret Mead served for more than forty years as a curator of the American Museum of Natural History in New York City.

full-page advertisement in *The New York Times* to wish Margaret Mead a happy birthday. The museum held a five day celebration in her honor.

In spite of her popularity, Margaret Mead often stirred up a great deal of controversy with her sometimes unconventional views. In an appearance before a Senate committee hearing on drugs, Mead urged that the use of marijuana be decriminalized.[4] On another occasion, she angered working women when she spoke out against the use of day care.[5]

During her long career, Mead wrote thirty-nine books, more than one thousand articles, and helped to produce numerous films and tapes. Margaret Mead made anthropology an understandable subject for all to enjoy.

Margaret Mead continued to be fully involved with life right up to the time of her death. When she discovered that she had a fatal form of cancer, Mead immediately began to keep records of the physical and mental changes that she experienced. In an obituary after her death on November 15, 1978, was the statement: "Of all the people she studied, few were as interesting as Margaret Mead herself."[6] In 1979, Margaret Mead was posthumously awarded the Presidential Medal of Freedom by President Jimmy Carter.

Ralph Bunche

5

Ralph Bunche
(1904–1971)

Ralph Bunche once said:

> I have a deepseated bias against hate and
> intolerance. I have a bias against racial and
> religious bigotry. I have a bias against war, a
> bias for peace. I have a bias which leads me
> to believe in the essential goodness of my
> fellow man, which leads me to believe that
> no problem in human relations is ever
> insoluble.[1]

True to his words, Bunche spent his life trying to
bring people and nations together, to live in peace.

Ralph Bunche was born in Detroit, Michigan,
on August 7, 1904, to Olive and Fred Bunche. The
African-American family, which also included one
daughter, lived in poverty in a Detroit ghetto. They
moved from Michigan to Albuquerque, New

41

Mexico, when Ralph was ten years old. Olive Bunche had tuberculosis, and the family hoped that the warmer climate in New Mexico would help her recover. Instead, her condition grew worse, and she died two years later, in 1916. Just three months later, Fred Bunche also died.

Twelve-year-old Ralph and his sister moved to Los Angeles, California, to live with their maternal grandmother, Lucy Johnson. She instilled in her grandchildren the importance of hard work and self-respect. Ralph Bunche later said that his grandmother was "the strongest woman I ever knew, even though she stood less than five feet high."[2]

Ralph Bunche lived up to Lucy Johnson's high expectations and graduated as valedictorian of his Jefferson High School class in 1922. After graduation, he enrolled in the University of California at Los Angeles, where an athletic scholarship helped pay for some of his college costs.

While in college, Bunche was a star guard on the basketball team and also played on the baseball and football teams. He participated in debate competitions and edited the sports section of the yearbook. He also studied international relations and graduated summa cum laude (with highest honors) in 1927. During his commencement address, Ralph Bunche urged the rest of his class to " . . . dedicate their lives to human fellowship and peace."[3]

Bunche received a scholarship to pursue graduate studies at Harvard University, but he could not afford the train fare to Cambridge, Massachusetts. An African-American women's club in Los Angeles donated $1,000 to help him with travel expenses. During his years in graduate school, Ralph Bunche studied government and received his master's degree in 1928. In that same year, Bunche moved to Washington, D.C., and joined the faculty of Howard University as a political science professor. While he was at Howard, one of his students, Ruth Harris, captured his attention and his heart. The couple married on June 23, 1930.

Additional graduate work at Harvard University earned a Ph.D. for Bunche in 1934. As part of his postgraduate studies at the University of Capetown, South Africa, Bunche conducted a field study in East Africa. He traveled to the Kenya highlands and lived among the Kikuyu tribe for three months, where he was named an honorary tribal citizen. When he traveled to other villages in the area, native drums announced his arrival, and he was honored with feasts and dancing.

After his field study was completed, Ralph Bunche returned to the United States and worked as an assistant to Swedish sociologist Gunnar Myrdal from 1938 to 1940. They studied bigotry and race relations in the United States and published their findings in a book called *An American Dilemma.* Bunche then returned to Howard University, where he taught until the United States entered World War II.

An old sports injury prevented Ralph Bunche from joining the armed forces, but he served in several government departments during World War II. His work involved the study of various colonial areas of the world in relation to their military importance to the United States. He also provided information about the people and customs in locales where American troops were stationed. His work eventually led to a position in the State Department, where he rose to the rank of acting chief of the Division of Dependent Area Affairs. He was the first African American to head a division in the State Department.

In 1946, Ralph Bunche left the State Department to join the newly founded United Nations (UN). He was the only African American to be a member of the United States delegation to the United Nations' first General Assembly. Trygve Lie, who was the UN secretary-general, hired Bunche to be the director of the trusteeship department, which helped former colonial territories prepare for self-government. In 1948, Lie asked Ralph Bunche to go to the Middle East with Count Folke Bernadotte of Sweden, a UN-appointed mediator.

Bernadotte was sent to the Middle East to try to resolve a conflict between Arabs and Jews who lived in Palestine. The conflict arose as a result of plans to divide Palestine into two states, one Arab and one Jewish. Arabs, who made up about 70 percent of the population of Palestine, opposed creation of the

Jewish state. Bombings and violent skirmishes were common in the area, and they escalated after the creation of the state of Israel in 1948. The UN mediators hoped to help resolve the conflict so that Arabs and Jews could live together peacefully in the Holy Land.

On September 17, 1948, Count Bernadotte was assassinated by Israeli terrorists, and Ralph Bunche took his place as chief UN negotiator. For the next eighty-one days, Bunche met with Arab and Jewish representatives on the island of Rhodes. With patience and tact, he arranged meetings and slowly earned the trust of the opposing parties. He was successful in negotiating an end to the conflict in 1949.

For his brilliant efforts on behalf of peace in the Middle East, Ralph Bunche was awarded the Nobel Peace Prize in 1950. He was the first African American to receive that honor. One of his colleagues said, "He's usually the first into a dangerous situation and the last out. He regards life with the calm and compassion of a selfless man devoted to a great task."[4]

During the next decade, Ralph Bunche was involved in other successful UN peacekeeping missions in Egypt and the Congo (now Zaire). After Belgium granted independence to the Congo in 1960, there was an absence of leadership in the emerging African nation. Bunche, along with twenty thousand United Nations forces, went to the struggling country to help maintain order and set up a government. His negotiations assisted in the

Ralph Bunche (right) meets with Dr. Martin Luther King, Jr., and Coretta Scott King in 1964. Bunche was always concerned with the cause of peace.

peaceful formation of the new country of Zaire. Ralph Bunche said about those efforts to help countries avoid further bloodshed, "For the first time, we have found a way to use military men for peace instead of war."[5]

From 1967 to 1971, Ralph Bunche served as UN undersecretary-general and was the highest American official in the United Nations. In recognition for his work in the areas of diplomacy and world peace, Ralph Bunche was awarded the Presidential Medal of Freedom by President Lyndon Johnson in 1963. President John Kennedy originally selected Bunche for the award, but Kennedy was assassinated before the ceremony could be held.

When Ralph Bunche was not involved in diplomatic negotiations, he spent time at home with his wife, Ruth, and their three children, Joan, Jane, and Ralph, Jr. He was a fan of baseball and football and liked to follow his favorite teams. Sometimes, during high-level meetings, messages were delivered to him. Instead of containing crucial information about the state of the world, the notes often listed the scores of the day's ball games.

As Ralph Bunche grew older, he began to have serious health problems. His years-long battle with diabetes had left his vision severely damaged. In addition, the disease weakened his kidneys and heart. Ralph Bunche did not give up his post, however, and remained undersecretary of the United Nations until just before his death on December 7, 1971.

Joe DiMaggio

6

Joe DiMaggio
(1914–   )

Joe DiMaggio once said, "When I was seven or eight, I picked up a broken paddle and started swinging. My sister Frances liked to pitch to me. They tell me I hit my sister's stuff pretty hard."[1] The shy boy from Martinez, California, would become one of baseball's greatest hitters.

Joseph Paul DiMaggio was born on November 25, 1914. He was the eighth of nine children born to Giuseppe and Rosalie DiMaggio, immigrants from Sicily. Joe's father was a fisherman, and the family spoke only Italian at home. Joe did not like the smell of fish, so he sold newspapers to make extra money rather than help his father on the boat. While he was a student at San Francisco Junior High School, Joe played on the baseball team.

Baseball skills seemed to run in the DiMaggio family. Two of Joe's older brothers, Dominic and Vincent, were professional baseball players. Joe sometimes skipped his junior high classes to watch his brothers play ball. By high school his interest in academics had all but disappeared. He quit school during his sophomore year and got a job in an orange juice cannery in the San Francisco area.

Joe's brother, Vince DiMaggio, played in the Pacific Coast League on a minor league team called the San Francisco Seals. In 1932, when his little brother was seventeen, Vince recommended that the team give Joe a chance. The Seals agreed, and during Joe's rookie year in 1933, he began a hitting streak. He had at least one hit in each of sixty-one games and batted .340 for the season. A good batting average is .300, which means that a player gets a hit three out of ten tries at bat.

In 1934, DiMaggio suffered a knee injury and missed most of the season but returned in 1935 to bat .398 and be named the Most Valuable Player (MVP) in the Pacific Coast League. Joe DiMaggio's incredible hitting soon attracted the attention of the major leagues. When the New York Yankees offered the Seals $25,000 and five players for DiMaggio, he signed with the team. Twenty-one-year-old Joe DiMaggio reported to major league training camp during the spring of 1936.

DiMaggio's rookie year performance with the Yankees earned him the nicknames "Yankee

Clipper" and "Joltin' Joe." He hit twenty-nine home runs and helped lead his team to victory in a World Series match-up with the New York Giants. When he was not slamming in home runs, DiMaggio did a fine job as the Yankee's center fielder.

The Yankees again won the World Series in 1937, the year DiMaggio hit forty-six home runs and batted .346. On June 13 of that year, Joltin' Joe hit three home runs in one game. Nothing could stop the Yankees as they captured the World Series title in 1938 and again in 1939. During those glory years, enthusiastic fans wildly cheered when Joe Di-Maggio stepped up to the plate. He rarely let his fans down and was named the Most Valuable Player in 1939, the year he batted .381. The year 1939 also saw the marriage of Joe DiMaggio and actress Dorothy Arnold.

During the 1941 baseball season, Joe DiMaggio began a hitting streak that lasted for fifty-six games. He had an incredible .408 batting average for the season and was again named the league's Most Valuable Player. Once again, the New York Yankees won the World Series in 1941. When he was asked to describe his hitting style, DiMaggio said, "I look for the pitcher's fast ball. Then, if he comes in with a curve, I still have time to swing."[2]

At the end of the 1942 season, Joe DiMaggio put down his bat and joined the Air Force. The United States had entered World War II after the bombing of Pearl Harbor on December 7, 1941.

DiMaggio was exempt from the service, yet he chose to trade his $43,000-a-year Yankee salary for $50 per month private's pay. He spent the next two and one-half years playing exhibition games for the troops.

When World War II ended, Joe DiMaggio returned to the Yankees. Even though his 1946 batting average of .290 was his worst ever, he quickly regained his professional skills. DiMaggio ended the 1947 season with a .315 average and another MVP award. That season would also see another World Series win for the Yankees.

Beginning in 1949, several physical ailments began to plague Joe DiMaggio. An injured arm and a foot problem caused him a great deal of pain. In spite of the fact that he missed several games due to his injuries, seventy thousand fans turned out for Joe DiMaggio Day at Yankee Stadium. They showered him with gifts and admiration, and he said to the crowd, "I want to thank the good Lord for making me a Yankee."[3]

During the 1951 season, DiMaggio continued to miss games due to injuries. He decided to retire from the Yankees after the team won the 1951 World Series. Joe DiMaggio played for the New York Yankees for thirteen seasons, and the team won the World Series ten times during those years. In his 1,736 games for the Yankees, he hit 361 home runs, struck out only 369 times, and had a lifetime batting average of .325.[4] Another baseball great, Ted Williams, once said, "DiMaggio even looks good striking out."[5]

When he announced his retirement, DiMaggio said:

> Old injuries have caught up with me, and I've had new ones. . . . I feel that I have reached the stage where I can no longer produce for my ball club, my manager, my teammates, and my fans the sort of baseball their loyalty to me deserves.[6]

Joe DiMaggio was quiet and shy as a boy, and remained so as an adult. An acquaintance of his once said that he was so reticent that if he said hello to you, that was a long conversation.[7] After his retirement, DiMaggio returned to San Francisco and worked as a broadcaster for just one season.

On January 14, 1954, Joe DiMaggio surprised many of his fans. Divorced from his first wife since 1944, DiMaggio married Marilyn Monroe, who was perhaps the most glamorous movie star of the time. The marriage lasted less than one year, but the couple remained close until Monroe's death.

In 1961, Joe DiMaggio returned to the Yankee camp for two weeks to serve as a coach and special assistant to the team's new manager, Ralph Houk. DiMaggio said:

> I'm here because I was asked for the first time. If I had been asked sooner, I probably would have come . . . Maybe I can help with fielding and base running. It's ridiculous to

Joe DiMaggio married Marilyn Monroe in 1954. Here, they are enjoying an evening out at New York's Stork Club.

think I can teach hitting in two weeks. I'll do whatever Houk wants me to do.[8]

During 1962, tragedy struck Joe DiMaggio's life when Marilyn Monroe died at the age of thirty-six. Even though eight years had passed since the couple's divorce, they had remained very close friends. DiMaggio helped Monroe's family plan the funeral. The grief-stricken DiMaggio shed tears as he walked behind Monroe's casket.[9]

After his retirement from the Yankees in 1951, Joe DiMaggio was elected to the Baseball Hall of Fame in 1955 and voted baseball's Greatest Living Player in a 1969 nationwide poll. In 1977, Joe Di-Maggio was awarded the Presidential Medal of Freedom by President Gerald Ford.

In 1994, a charity baseball game was held in Ft. Lauderdale, Florida. Joe DiMaggio was there to reminisce about his glory years with the Yankees. Recalling those days, he said, "I loved being at the Stadium. I always got there early, and I was never in a rush to leave. We played afternoons then. When the game was over, I took my time. Why rush into the night?"[10]

Now in his eighties, Joe DiMaggio is retired and lives in southern Florida. He still makes public appearances and signs autographs for his many fans.

Hector Garcia

Hector Garcia
(1914–   )

On June 6, 1995, one hundred and fifty people gathered on the grounds of the Corpus Christi branch of Texas A & M University. They were there to pay tribute to eighty-one-year-old Hector Garcia and to dedicate an outdoor site to honor his accomplishments. The small park is shaded by trees and dotted with benches and a gazebo. A nine-foot-tall bronze statue of Hector Garcia is the focal point of the area.

After the ground-breaking ceremony, Garcia said:

> I feel what I did, I owe to other people. I owe it to my family, who stood behind me, and of course to the American GI Forum, who gave me backing, and to the Lord that gave me the energy to keep up the work that I did.[1]

Hector Garcia dedicated his life to helping the Hispanic-American residents of Corpus Christi, Texas, and the surrounding towns.

Life began for Hector Garcia on January 17, 1914, when he was born in Llera, Mexico, to Jose and Faustina Garcia. Hector's father was a professor, and he stressed the importance of education to his seven children. When the family fled the Mexican Revolution in 1918, they settled in Mercedes, Texas, and operated a general store.

A few months after his high school graduation, Hector Garcia entered the University of Texas, where he earned a bachelor's degree in zoology in 1936. Four years later, he graduated from the University of Texas Medical School. He then spent two years of surgical internship in Omaha, Nebraska, at St. Joseph's Hospital.

As soon as Garcia finished his medical education in 1942, he joined the United States Army. The United States had entered World War II after the bombing of Pearl Harbor, on December 7, 1941. Garcia was sent to Europe where he served as a combat surgeon in the infantry and medical corps. It was during a tour of duty in Naples, Italy, that Garcia met Wanda Fusillo, an Italian student at the University of Naples.

Although he was sent to Germany, the couple exchanged letters until Garcia's return to Italy in June 1945. Hector Garcia and Wanda Fusillo were married on June 23, 1945, just after Wanda was awarded a doctoral degree in liberal arts. The Garcias would eventually have three daughters and one son. Hector Garcia's service in the military earned him a

Bronze Star and six Battle Stars, and he was discharged with the rank of major in the Medical Corps.

After his military duty, Hector Garcia set up a medical practice in Corpus Christi, Texas. In the beginning, the physician could not afford a car and had to take the bus when he made house calls. Many of his patients were Hispanic-American veterans who complained that the government was not providing the medical and educational assistance that had been promised. The veterans were entitled to financial aid under a program called the GI Bill of Rights.

On March 26, 1948, Garcia presided over a meeting in Corpus Christi to address the veterans' problems and founded the American GI Forum that same night. The purpose of the organization was to help Hispanic-American veterans get the medical and educational benefits that were due to them. It also encouraged its members to become involved in the local community and in political activities. By July 1948, Hector Garcia helped establish eleven additional chapters of the GI Forum in surrounding towns. An incident early in 1949 brought national attention to the group.

A former Corpus Christi resident, Felix Longoria, was killed in action during World War II. In 1949, his remains were finally shipped to Texas for burial. A local funeral director refused to allow Longoria's family the use of the chapel. He said, "I'm sorry, but we don't let Mexicans use our chapel and we don't intend to let them start now."[2]

To protest the racist decision, Hector Garcia wrote letters to several elected officials. Within twenty-four hours, he received a telegram from Lyndon B. Johnson, who was then United States senator from Texas. Johnson wrote:

> I deeply regret to learn that the prejudice of some individuals extends even beyond this life. I have no authority over civilian funeral homes. However, I have today made arrangements to have Felix Longoria buried with full military honors in Arlington National Cemetery here at Washington where the honored dead of our nation's wars rest.[3]

The fallen soldier was buried on February 16, 1949, in a ceremony that was attended by the Longoria family along with Senator Johnson.

When he was not involved with the activities of the GI Forum, Hector Garcia had his growing medical practice to occupy him. He often stayed in the office late into the evening. Garcia's daughter Wanda said later, "He certainly had more energy than anyone I've ever met in my life."[4]

Hector Garcia's patients included the poorest Hispanic-American residents of Corpus Christi. Many of them could not pay for their office visits and medicine. Garcia treated them anyway and was often called the "doctor of the poor." He once said about some of his patients, "I've been asked why it is that I'm so interested in those people. It is because those people are my people. I, like they, suffered in poverty and knew hunger."[5]

Through the years, Hector Garcia was also involved with the League of Latin American Citizens (LULAC), which was established in 1929 to seek economic, educational, and political equality for Hispanic Americans. Work with the GI Forum and LULAC gave Garcia a reputation on the national level. His involvement in the presidential campaigns of John F. Kennedy in 1960 and Lyndon Johnson in 1964 helped attract the Hispanic-American vote to those candidates. In 1956 and 1960, he served on the Democratic National Committee, and in 1960, he also helped organize "Viva Kennedy" clubs to garner support for John F. Kennedy.

In 1967, Hector Garcia was named by President Lyndon Johnson to be an alternate delegate to the United Nations, with the rank of ambassador. Johnson also appointed him to be the first Hispanic American to serve on the United States Commission on Civil Rights. Hector Garcia's political activity did not make everyone happy. He received hate mail and death threats, but he was not deterred by them. He later said about the threats, "I didn't advertise everything I was doing. In other words, if I went to fight school discrimination in the next town, I wouldn't publicize that. And I would never come back the same way I left."[6]

Hector Garcia organized "Viva Kennedy" clubs in 1960 to help garner Hispanic support for John F. Kennedy's campaign. Garcia is shown here with President Kennedy in 1961.

The years have not slowed the pace of Hector Garcia. He still spends several hours each day in his office. One of his patients said:

> Everybody knew that he was the doctor who would take care of you and make sure nothing went wrong. More than just physically. He was the person you could trust. There was never anybody else, just Doctor Hector.[7]

In 1984, President Ronald Reagan awarded Hector Garcia the Presidential Medal of Freedom.

When the Corpus Christi Memorial Medical Center dedicated a health center in Hector Garcia's name, Senator Edward Kennedy of Massachusetts wrote: "Whether the issue is civil rights or medical care or foreign policy, America has gained immeasurably from Dr. Garcia's contributions which span more than half a century of courageous leadership."[8]

Hector Garcia does not spend all of his time seeing patients and trying to correct the problems of Hispanic Americans. For twenty-five years, he has met with a group of friends on Saturday nights to play dominoes. Joe Ramos, who has been a part of the game for many years, said about Garcia: "He usually wins more than any [of the] other guys. I guess he's just got a little more luck."[9]

Now in his eighties, Hector Garcia is often in poor health. Once he recovers his strength, though, he goes right back to his office to examine the dozens of patients who depend on him every day.

Cesar Chavez

Cesar Chavez
(1927–1993)

Cesar Estrada Chavez was born on March 31, 1927, in Yuma, Arizona, the second son of Librado and Juana Estrada Chavez's six children. In 1937, when Cesar was ten years old, his family had to give up their one-hundred-acre homestead. Even though the Chavez family had worked very hard on the poor land, they were not able to make enough money to pay taxes on the property. Because they had no place to go, Cesar's parents and their five children became migrant workers, traveling from one harvesting job to another in Arizona and California.

The work was brutal. Migrant workers, who were mostly Hispanic Americans and Mexican citizens, spent long hours in the fields, stooping to pick grapes, strawberries, or other ripe produce. The sun beat down on their heads, while insects swarmed around their dusty bodies. At the end of an exhausting day, the only shelter available to the family was usually a one-room shack with no water or electricity.

Cesar's brother, Richard, remembered the first winter that the family was on the road. Their father took a job in Oxnard, California, picking lima beans. Eventually all of the beans were gathered, and no more work was available. The small amount of money that the family had earned quickly disappeared, and they had nowhere to stay. A kind lady offered the Chavez family use of an empty field that she owned. They pitched a very small tent, and all crowded in for the winter.

Richard Chavez said, "All the family stayed there. And it rained that winter. Oh, it rained. Rain, rain, rain. We had to go to school barefoot. We had no shoes. I can't forget it."[1] That entire winter, the family ate only beans and tortillas.

Because migrant farm work was seasonal, it was very difficult to find employment for more than six months a year. In addition, migrant workers had no insurance benefits or pension plans. They could be fired at any time. Many laborers crossed the border from Mexico and were eager to work in the United States. As bad as conditions were here, they were even worse in Mexico.

The nomadic lives of the migrant workers made it difficult for the children to attend school. Cesar Chavez went to more than sixty schools, a week at one, a month at another, and only completed seventh grade. When the crops were ripe, the family had to work, even if school was in session. Chavez remembered "walking barefoot to school through the mud, fishing in the canals for wild mustard greens to ward off starvation, collecting tinfoil from empty cigarette packages to sell to a junk dealer for a sweatshirt or a pair of shoes."[2]

When Cesar was about thirteen years old, a union began to organize the farm workers. Cesar's father and uncle joined the union and participated in a strike by carrying picket signs at a dried-fruit company in San Jose, California. The union men sometimes met at the Chavez home to talk about their hopes for higher wages and better working conditions. Young Cesar listened to the discussions and later said, "It made a deep impression on me."[3]

In 1944, when Chavez was just seventeen years old, he joined the United States Navy and served until World War II ended in 1945. When he was discharged from the Navy, Chavez once again became a migrant worker. He was living in Delano, California, and working in the surrounding vineyards when he married Helen Fabela in 1948. The couple would have eight children in the years ahead.

In 1952, Cesar Chavez joined the Community Service Organization (CSO) in San Jose, California. The CSO tried to assist migrant workers and other disadvantaged people with their housing, medical, and legal problems. Chavez conducted many voter registration drives among the migrant workers. During his time with CSO, Chavez learned valuable lessons about leadership and organization. His successful volunteer work led to a paid position with the group in 1954 and the title of CSO director for California and Arizona in 1958.

While he was an employee with the CSO, Chavez wanted to organize the farm workers into a union. The CSO did not agree with his plan, so Chavez left the organization in 1962. He took his savings of $1,200 and began to organize the National Farm Workers Association (NFWA) in Delano, California. Area farm owners threatened to fire any workers who joined the NFWA. Chavez drove all over the San Joaquin Valley, talking to migrant workers about their poor wages and working conditions. He told them, "We are free men and we demand justice."[4] Chavez and his followers held nonviolent protest marches and sing-ins to dramatize the plight of the farm laborers.

By 1965, the NFWA had seventeen hundred members enrolled, and the union joined with the Filipino grape pickers' strike. They demanded that the three largest California grape growers raise the pay of the farm workers to $1.40 an hour. When the growers refused, Cesar Chavez asked Americans to stop buying table grapes that did not have a union label. He also staged a twenty-five-day hunger strike.

Union representatives from the NFWA traveled across the United States and talked to community leaders about the grape boycott. Chavez said:

> Our strikers have been under the gun, they
> have been kicked and beaten and herded by
> dogs, they have been cursed and ridiculed,
> they have been stripped and chained and
> jailed, they have been sprayed with the
> poisons used in the vineyards.[5]

As the strike, or "la huelga," continued, the grape
boycott gradually spread across the United States.
Mayors in many large cities directed their purchas-
ing agents not to buy table grapes that were grown
in California. The boycott began to hurt the vine-
yard owners, and by 1969, sales of table grapes were
down 12 percent and 140 out of 200 Delano area
grape growers had gone bankrupt.[6]

In 1970, many of the growers decided to meet
the union's demands. They raised wages and issued
three-year contracts to their farm workers. Then, in
1973, many of the grape producers decided not to
renew the contracts, and Chavez had to redouble his
efforts in the fight for better worker conditions.

In the early 1970s, Cesar Chavez moved the
union headquarters and his large family to La Paz,
California. Chavez took only $10 a week for his
work as president of the union. Membership dues
that had been collected over the years were used to
build a library, chapel, and a meeting hall on the
property. A credit union for the members was
organized and operated by Helen Fabela Chavez.

During the 1980s, Cesar Chavez used the media
to inform people of the still terrible conditions of

Cesar Chavez organized a strike to boycott California grapes. He hoped to raise the pay of migrant workers.

many of the migrant workers. Through letters and television, he tried to increase support for his organization, which later came to be called the United Farm Workers (UFW). In 1988, Chavez again staged a hunger strike. He fasted to call attention to the use of pesticides on farm produce.

In 1992, Chavez accompanied reporters on a tour of a California citrus grove during harvest time. He showed them that many of the workers still made as little as $2.50 an hour and had to pay to sleep in the grove at night. Adding to their problems, there is evidence that migrant workers who spend their days harvesting crops have a higher incidence of cancer.[7] They are in daily contact with a large number of pesticides.

Cesar Chavez continued to fight for the rights of farm workers. When he died on April 23, 1993, the sixty-six-year-old union organizer was engaged in yet another hunger strike. Chavez once said, "There is no life apart from the union. If the union falls apart when I am gone, I will have been a miserable failure."[8]

On April 29, 1993, Cesar Chavez was buried in Delano, California. Twenty-five thousand mourners attended his funeral. During the year after his death, membership in the UFW rose to one hundred thousand. In a White House ceremony in 1994, the Presidential Medal of Freedom was awarded posthumously to Cesar Chavez by President Bill Clinton.

Neil Armstrong

Neil Armstrong
(1930–   )

"Houston, Tranquility Base here. The *Eagle* has landed!"[1]

On July 19, 1969, astronauts Neil Armstrong and Edwin "Buzz" Aldrin landed safely on the surface of the Moon. The incredible feat was the culmination of more than eight years of intense effort on the part of the National Aeronautics and Space Administration (NASA). On May 25, 1961, President John F. Kennedy had said, "I believe that this nation should commit itself to achieving the goal, before this decade is out, of landing a man on the Moon and returning him safely to Earth."[2]

Less than ten years later, not one, but two Americans were in the lunar module *Eagle,* preparing to open the hatch. Neil Armstrong, as commander of the *Apollo 11* mission, would be first down the ladder. He would take his place in history as the first person ever to step onto the surface of the Moon. What events in Armstrong's life had led him to be a part of this amazing feat?

Stephen and Viola Armstrong's son, Neil, was born on August 5, 1930, in Wapakoneta, Ohio. When he was six years old, Neil took his first airplane ride and fell in love with aviation. He read about flying, built model airplanes, and began taking flying lessons at age fourteen. On his sixteenth birthday, in 1946, Neil Armstrong earned his pilot's license before he even had his driver's license.

After Armstrong graduated from Wapakoneta High School in 1947, he entered Purdue University, located in West Lafayette, Indiana, to study aeronautical engineering. He was a Naval Air Cadet while in college and was called to active duty in 1949, after his sophomore year. After flight training in Pensacola, Florida, Armstrong earned his wings and was sent to fight in the Korean War, where he flew seventy-eight missions. On one of those missions, Armstrong's jet fighter was hit by enemy fire. He flew the severely damaged aircraft across Allied lines and then safely ejected. For his bravery and skill as a fighter pilot, Neil Armstrong received three Air Medals.

After serving in the Navy, Armstrong returned to Purdue, where he earned his degree in aeronautical engineering in 1955. He became a civilian test pilot and helped check out airplanes that were in various stages of development. He logged more than one thousand hours as he flew the F-100, F-104, B-47, F-102, and X-15 rocket planes. In the X-15, Neil Armstrong sometimes flew at an altitude of forty miles and at speeds up to four thousand miles per hour. One of his friends said, "He flies an airplane like he's wearing it."[3]

After seven years as a test pilot, Armstrong volunteered for NASA's astronaut training program and was accepted in 1962. He and Janet Shearon had married in 1956 and were the parents of two sons and a daughter. The daughter had died before she was three years old. The family packed up their belongings and moved to Clear Lake City, Texas, site of NASA and the astronaut training facility. At the time that Armstrong reported for duty, the United States was engaged in a race with the Soviet Union to conquer space.

On April 12, 1961, Soviet cosmonaut Yuri Gagarin became the first person in space. The United States quickly followed suit, and on May 5, 1961, launched Navy Commander Alan B. Shepard 115 miles into space. Soviet cosmonaut Gherman Titov became the first person to orbit Earth on August 17, 1961. Six months later, Lieutenant Colonel John Glenn was the first American sent into orbit. As the race to conquer space continued, NASA shifted into higher and higher gears.

Project Mercury flights were followed by Project Gemini, which was a bridge to the Apollo program and the Moon. During the Gemini flights, docking maneuvers were practiced, and the astronauts took their first walks in space. As Neil Armstrong and David Scott attempted to perform the first manual docking maneuver on *Gemini 8,* disaster struck. Their spacecraft was sent into a near-fatal spin when a jet thruster on the Agena target vehicle malfunctioned. As *Gemini 8* tumbled out of control, Armstrong calmly unlocked the Agena from the spacecraft and used the reentry rockets to control the spin.

After the Gemini missions were completed, Project Apollo got underway. Apollo missions one through six were unmanned flights that tested the vehicles and equipment that would take astronauts to the Moon. Apollo missions seven through ten carried astronauts who performed all of the maneuvers that would be necessary for the project to succeed. Finally, with all of the equipment in order and the training completed, the time arrived to actually land astronauts on the surface of the Moon.

On January 9, 1969, the crew of the *Apollo 11* mission was announced. On board would be thirty-eight-year-old Neil Armstrong as the civilian commander of the mission, along with thirty-nine-year-old Colonel Edwin "Buzz" Aldrin and thirty-eight-year-old Lieutenant Colonel Michael Collins. Armstrong and Aldrin would descend to the Moon's surface, while Collins orbited in the command module *Columbia.*

On July 16, 1969, the three-man flight crew ate breakfast, dressed in their spacesuits, and made their way to the launch site. Neil Armstrong said:

> All was ready. Everything had been done. Projects Mercury and Gemini. Seven years of Project Apollo. The work of more than 300,000 Americans. . . . The time had come. . . . As we ascended in the elevator to the top of the Saturn on the morning of July 16, 1969, we knew that hundreds of thousands of Americans had given their best effort to give us this chance. Now it was time for us to give our best.[4]

The 363-foot-tall Saturn 5 rocket blasted off at 9:32 A.M. EDT as 1 million spectators watched from the beaches and roads around Cape Kennedy, Florida. Two and one-half hours later, *Apollo 11* broke from Earth's gravity and began a 238,857-mile, 3-day voyage to the Moon. On July 19, the spacecraft entered the Moon's gravity and went into lunar orbit. At that point, Armstrong and Aldrin crawled through a narrow hatchway that linked the command module to the lunar module *Eagle.*

Once inside *Eagle,* the astronauts fired a rocket that would propel them toward the surface of the Moon. When the *Eagle* was three hundred feet from the landing site, the crew saw that they were headed right for an area filled with large boulders. Neil Armstrong disconnected the computer, took over manual control of the landing, and looked for a safer surface. With only twenty seconds of fuel left, the *Eagle* finally planted four flimsy legs on the surface of the Moon.

Six and one-half hours later, the astronauts opened the hatch, and Neil Armstrong began his historic descent down the ladder. A television camera that was mounted on the outside of the lunar module transmitted fuzzy pictures back to Earth. Millions of viewers worldwide breathlessly watched as Neil Armstrong stepped onto the Moon's surface and then said, "That's one small step for a man . . . one giant leap for mankind."[5]

Edwin "Buzz" Aldrin soon joined his fellow astronaut, and the men set to work. They were dressed in 185-pound suits that provided water, oxygen, and refrigeration, as well as two-way radios so that they could communicate. The astronauts set up an additional television camera and various equipment for scientific studies. They collected samples of Moon rocks and soil and carefully packed them in sealed, airtight containers. Scientists hoped to learn much about the Moon and its origin from these lunar rocks and soil. Also, the astronauts left an engraved plaque on the Moon that read: "Here Men from the planet Earth first set foot upon the Moon, July 1969 A.D. We came in peace for all mankind."[6]

After spending twenty-one hours and thirty-seven minutes on the Moon's surface, the *Eagle* blasted off to rendezvous with Michael Collins in the command module. On July 22, 1969, *Columbia*'s main engines were fired, and *Apollo 11* began its trip back home. The spacecraft safely splashed down in the Pacific Ocean on July 24, and the crew was picked up and flown to the U.S.S. *Hornet,* an aircraft carrier that was waiting for them.

The men spent three weeks in quarantine after their arrival from the Moon. The possibility existed that the astronauts were contaminated with some unknown bacteria from the lunar surface. While they were quarantined, doctors examined the men and the rock and soil samples that were recovered from the Moon. Once they were declared to be safe, Neil Armstrong, Michael Collins, and Edwin "Buzz" Aldrin emerged from their mobile quarantine facility to face a heroes' welcome in the United States. The three astronauts were honored in parades and embarked on a worldwide tour. Neil Armstrong was awarded the Presidential Medal of Freedom by President Richard Nixon in 1969, along with his fellow astronauts, Michael Collins and Edwin "Buzz" Aldrin.

After the excitement of *Apollo 11* died down, Neil Armstrong served as the deputy associate administrator for aeronautics at NASA until 1971. At that time, he retired from the space agency and moved to Ohio, where he taught engineering at the University of Cincinnati until 1979. Since that time, he has been the chairman of a defense electronics firm and a computer company executive. He lives on a farm in Ohio and does not often grant interviews.

The *Apollo 11* astronauts spent three weeks in quarantine after their arrival from the Moon. From left to right: Neil Armstrong, Michael Collins, Edwin "Buzz" Aldrin, and President Richard Nixon.

After the successful *Apollo 11* mission, Neil Armstrong said:

> The single thing which makes any man happiest is the realization that he has worked up to the limits of his ability, his capacity. It's all the better, of course, if this work has made a contribution to knowledge, or toward moving the human race a little farther forward."[7]

Colin Powell

Colin Powell
(1937–   )

When Colin Powell was a freshman at City College of New York in 1954, he admired the uniforms that some Reserve Officer Training Corps (ROTC) students were wearing. The ROTC introduced its members to military philosophy and discipline. Colin Powell joined the organization and later said, "I liked ROTC. It had to do with the guys around me, the sense of order that the military brought to my life. When you find something you're good at, you tend to pursue it."[1] Powell excelled in the ROTC and achieved the rank of cadet colonel by his graduation in 1958.

Life began for Colin Powell on April 5, 1937, in Harlem, a neighborhood in New York City. Luther and Maud Powell, who were also the parents of a daughter, Marilyn, were immigrants from the

Caribbean island of Jamaica. In the past, their ancestors had been brought from Africa to the island to serve as slaves. When Colin was still a child, the family moved to the Bronx, a borough of New York City. Powell said, "I had a great childhood. We lived in a tenement neighborhood in a big extended family. I didn't know I was a minority because everybody there was a minority."[2]

Even though Powell's parents had not graduated from high school, they stressed education and filled their small home with many books. Colin played stickball with the other boys in the neighborhood and worked after school at a baby furniture store. He was an average student who graduated from Morris High School in 1954. After four years at City College, Colin Powell earned a bachelor's degree in geology and graduated at the top of his 1958 ROTC class.

On July 9, 1958, Powell was commissioned a second lieutenant in the United States Army and reported for basic training at Fort Benning, Georgia. His early military career included two tours of duty in Vietnam during the 1960s. On one of his missions in Vietnam, the helicopter in which Powell was riding crashed. Unhurt, Powell escaped from the aircraft and began to run. Realizing that his crewmates were injured, he returned to the crash site and rescued four of the men who were trapped inside the smoking helicopter. Those rescues, along with other acts of valor in Vietnam, earned for Colin Powell a Purple Heart, a Bronze Star, and a Soldier's Medal.

After his tours in Vietnam, Colin Powell returned to the United States to join his wife, Alma Johnson Powell, whom he had married in 1962. While he was serving in Vietnam, the couple's first child, Michael, was born on March 23, 1963. Just two years later, daughter Linda was born on April 16, 1965.

During the early 1970s, Powell earned a master's degree in business administration and was promoted to the rank of army major. In 1971, Colin Powell was chosen to be a White House Fellow in Washington, D.C. The fellowship provided an opportunity for him to work closely with a top government official for a year. Powell spent his year as an assistant to Frank Carlucci, deputy director of the Office of Management and Budget. During his year as a White House Fellow, the Powell's third child, Anne Marie, was born on May 20, 1971.

In 1972, Colin Powell was sent to Korea as a battalion commander. He returned to Pentagon duty in 1974 and attended the National War College the following year, where he graduated with honors in 1976. For the next ten years, Powell continued to rise in rank and alternated duty between various army bases and Washington, D.C.

In 1981, Powell was serving as deputy commander at Fort Leavenworth, Kansas, when Secretary of Defense Caspar Weinberger asked him to be his senior military advisor. Powell spent four years in that position and was then sent to West

Germany as the commander of the Fifth Corps. After only a year in Germany, Powell was once again summoned to Washington.

Beginning in 1987, Colin Powell served as the second-in-command to National Security Advisor Frank Carlucci, his boss from the military budget office. When Carlucci was promoted to secretary of defense in 1987, President Ronald Reagan named Colin Powell as the new national security advisor. As part of his duties, Powell worked closely with the White House and the military during the successful United States invasions of Grenada and Panama.

After his tenure as national security advisor was over, Colin Powell reported for duty at Fort McPherson, Georgia, where he became head of all of the army ground forces in the continental United States. Powell said about his time with the troops, "It's great being a commander in the field, where you set your own agenda and are close to the soldiers. That keeps you young."[3] Colin Powell would not have long to spend with the men and women in the field, though.

In 1989, President George Bush nominated Powell to be chairman of the Joint Chiefs of Staff (JCS). Bush said, "As we face the challenges of the 90s, it is most important that the Chairman of the Joint Chiefs of Staff be a person of breadth, judgement, experience, and total integrity. Colin Powell has all those qualities and more."[4] The Senate agreed, and on September 22, 1989, voted to approve the Powell nomination. After his confirmation, former Defense Secretary Caspar Weinberger said about Colin Powell, "He is one of the very best persons I have ever worked with in any of the positions I've had."[5]

When Colin Powell assumed his responsibilities as chairman of the Joint Chiefs of Staff he became the youngest person ever to hold that office and the only African American. The JCS is made up of the heads of the Army, Navy, Marine Corps, and Air Force, in addition to the chairman and vice-chairman. Their duty is to advise the president and his secretary of defense about military matters. With Colin Powell as chairman, the six-person group met three times a week in a tightly guarded room.

It was in that room that talks concerning Iraqi president Saddam Hussein's 1990 invasion of Kuwait were discussed. When President George Bush decided to send American forces to try to get the Iraqis out of Kuwait and to stop them from invading Saudi Arabia, the Joint Chiefs assisted in the planning. Thousands of United States troops were moved into position, and Iraq was given until January 15, 1991, to withdraw from Kuwait. When the deadline passed with no withdrawal, Operation Desert Storm began.

On January 16, 1991, massive air strikes were launched by United States and coalition forces against Hussein's army. The aerial bombardment continued for five weeks, during which time there were many Iraqi casualties and desertions. After the air strikes had done their damage, ground troops were sent into the Iraqi-occupied territory on February 23, 1991. The ground assault, which lasted only four days, smashed what was left of Saddam Hussein's army and liberated Kuwait City.

During the weeks of the Persian Gulf War, United States and Iraqi troop movements were followed closely by the news media. Press briefings from Saudi Arabia and Washington were televised daily, and Colin Powell spent a great deal of time in front of the camera. America got to know Powell as he conducted his daily briefings, and he became a recognizable figure to many in this country.

After the successful completion of the Persian Gulf War, articles about Colin Powell appeared in many periodicals. Along with his soaring approval ratings came talk of a possible presidential candidacy. During this time, Colin Powell made the decision to step down as chairman of the Joint Chiefs of Staff and retire from military life. In a farewell to the JCS, he said, "I am where I am today because the army takes care of its own. I was allowed to rise based on performance."[6] Colin Powell had served his country with honor and dignity for more than thirty-five years and retired from active military service with the rank of four-star general.

In 1991, Colin Powell was invited to the White House where he was awarded the Presidential Medal of Freedom by President George Bush. The ceremony

General Colin Powell speaks at a Pentagon briefing about Operation Desert Storm, on January 23, 1991.

was repeated in 1993, when Powell was given a second Presidential Medal of Freedom by President Bill Clinton. Only once before had anyone been awarded two of the medals. That was diplomat Ellsworth Bunker, who received the Presidential Medal of Freedom in 1963 and 1968.

When Colin Powell retired from active military duty, he did not stop being productive. Powell had always visited schools to talk to the students about the importance of a good education, and he increased those visits after his retirement. In his spare time, Powell restores antique Volvos at the suburban Washington, D.C., home that he shares with his wife, Alma. Their three children are grown, but the Powells now have two grandsons to entertain and enjoy.

In the fall of 1995, Colin Powell's autobiography, *An American Journey,* was published, and he embarked on a nationwide tour to discuss and promote the book. Powell's appearances at a number of bookstores across the country drew large crowds of people. Many stood in line for hours to get a chance to meet Powell and have him autograph a copy of the book. A large number of people also asked Powell about his plans for the upcoming presidential race.

After his successful book tour, Colin Powell returned to his home to make an important decision. During the last week of October 1995, he gathered his family and trusted advisors around him to discuss a possible run for the White House. Powell's family was worried about his safety and their own loss of privacy. It was a difficult decision to make and Colin Powell told a friend "I'm struggling."[7]

Finally, after much thought and prayer, Colin Powell announced that he would not be entering the 1996 presidential race. He said: "To offer myself as a candidate for president requires a commitment and a passion . . . Such a life requires a calling that I do not yet hear."[8] After the decision was made, Powell's niece, Lisa Berns, asked her uncle how he felt. "Like a weight has been lifted off my shoulders," Colin Powell answered.[9]

Chapter Notes

Preface

1. Ken Adelman, "Ground Zero," *Washingtonian,* April 30, 1990, p. 69.

Chapter 1

1. Helen Keller, *The Story of My Life* (Garden City, N.Y.: Doubleday & Co., 1954) (originally published 1903), p. 26.

2. Ibid., p. 34.

3. Ibid., p. 16.

4. Ibid., p. 36.

5. Barbara Sicherman and others, eds., *Notable American Women* (Cambridge, Mass.: Harvard University Press, 1980), p. 390.

6. Keller, p. 47.

7. Maxine Block, ed., "Helen Keller," in *Current Biography Yearbook 1942* (New York: H.W. Wilson Company, 1942), p. 444.

Chapter 2

1. Michael Kernan, "The Object at Hand," *Smithsonian,* June 1993, p. 16.

2. Maxine Block, ed., "Marian Anderson," in *Current Biography Yearbook 1940* (New York: H.W. Wilson Company, 1940), p. 18

3. Ibid.

4. Barbara Carlisle Bigelow, ed., *Contemporary Black Biography,* Vol. 2 (Detroit: Gale Research, 1992), p. 7.

5. Kernan, p. 16.

6. Ibid.

7. Katrine Ames, "She Let Freedom Ring," *Newsweek,* April 19, 1993, p. 73.

8. Marian Anderson, *My Lord, What a Morning* (New York: Viking Press, 1956), p. 199.

9. Bigelow, p. 6.

10. Ibid., pp. 5–6.

11. "The Beacon," *Newsweek,* April 26, 1965, p. 87.

12. Bigelow, p. 5.

13. Rosalyn M. Story, "Marian Anderson, 1897–1993," *Opera News,* July 1993, p. 55.

14. Anderson, p. 158.

Chapter 3

1. Alberta Gould, *First Lady of the Senate* (Mt. Desert, Maine: Windswept House Publishers, 1990), p. 63.

2. "As Maine Goes . . . ," *Time,* September 5, 1960, p. 15.

3. Charles Moritz, ed., "Margaret Chase Smith," in *Current Biography Yearbook 1962* (New York: H.W. Wilson Co., 1962), p. 395.

4. "As Maine Goes . . . ," p. 15.

5. "A Woman for President?" *U.S. News and World Report,* February 10, 1964, p. 36.

6. Ibid., pp. 35–36.

7. Ibid., p. 36.

8. *Congress A to Z* (Washington, D.C.: Congressional Quarterly, 1993), pp. 432, 434.

9. "Margaret Chase Smith, Political Pioneer, Is Dead," *Houston Chronicle,* May 30, 1995, p. A7.

Chapter 4

1. "She Spoke Her Mind," *Newsweek,* November 27, 1978, p. 75.

2. Jacqueline Ludel, *Margaret Mead* (New York: Franklin Watts, 1983), p. 22.

3. Phyllis Rose, ed., *The Norton Book of Women's Lives* (New York: W.W. Norton & Company, 1993), p. 555.

4. "Margaret Mead: 1901–1978," *Time,* November 27, 1978, p. 57.

5. "She Spoke Her Mind," p. 75.

6. "Margaret Mead: 1901–1978," p. 57.

Chapter 5

1. Barbara Carlisle Bigelow, ed., *Contemporary Black Biography,* Vol. 5 (Detroit: Gale Research, 1992), p. 43.

2. Anna Rothe, ed., "Ralph Bunche" in *Current Biography Yearbook 1948* (New York: H.W. Wilson Co., 1948), p. 77.

3. Bigelow, p. 42.

4. Ibid., p. 43.

5. "A Man Without Color," *Time,* December 20, 1971, p. 34.

Chapter 6

1. Roger Kahn, *The Era: 1947–1957* (New York: Ticknor & Fields, 1993), p. 70.

2. Anna Rothe, ed., "Joe DiMaggio" in *Current Biography Yearbook 1951* (New York: H.W. Wilson Co., 1951), p. 163.

3. Ibid.

4. *Great Athletes,* Vol. 5 (Pasadena, Calif.: Salem Press, 1992), p. 627.

5. Geoffrey C. Ward & Ken Burns, "Joe DiMaggio," *U.S. News & World Report,* August 29, 1994, p. 89.

6. Rothe, p. 164.

7. Ward & Burns, p. 89.

8. "No. 5 Returns," *Newsweek,* March 20, 1961, p. 89.

9. "I Love You . . . I Love You . . . ," *Newsweek,* August 20, 1962, p. 31.

10. Mike Lupica, "The Eternal Yankee," *Esquire,* May 1994, p. 52.

Chapter 7

1. Charlott Huff, "Hector Garcia Plaza Seen as Inspiration for Students," *Corpus Christi Caller-Times,* June 2, 1995, p. B1.

2. Tyrone Meighan, "Helping Veterans, Many More," *Corpus Christi Caller-Times,* July 3, 1993, p. F10.

3. Ibid., p. F11.

4. Tyrone Meighan, "Dr. Hector P. Garcia," *Corpus Christi Caller-Times,* July 3, 1993, p. F3.

5. Tyrone Meighan, "Dr. as Doctor," *Corpus Christi Caller-Times,* July 3, 1993, p. F9.

6. Meighan, "Dr. Hector P. Garcia," p. F4.

7. Meighan, "Dr. as Doctor," p. F9.

8. Meighan, "Dr. Hector P. Garcia," p. F4.

9. Tyrone Meighan, "A Demon at Dominoes," *Corpus Christi Caller-Times,* July 3, 1993, p. F15.

Chapter 8

1. "The Little Strike That Grew to *La Causa,*" *Time,* July 4, 1969, p. 20.

2. Charles Moritz, ed., "Cesar Chavez," in *Current Biography Yearbook 1969* (New York: H.W. Wilson Co., 1969), p. 87.

3. Ibid.

4. "The Little Strike That Grew to *La Causa,*" p. 17.

5. Susan Sinnott, *Extraordinary Hispanic Americans* (Chicago: Childrens Press, 1991), p. 188.

6. David Gates, "A Secular Saint of the '60s," *Newsweek,* May 3, 1993, p. 68.

7. Ron Karten, "Grape Wars," *Progressive,* July 1992, p. 14.

8. Gates, p. 68.

Chapter 9

1. Edgar M. Cortwright, ed., *Apollo Expeditions to the Moon* (Washington, D.C.: National Aeronautics and Space Administration, 1975), p. 212.

2. Ibid., p. 18.

3. Charles Moritz, ed., "Neil Armstrong," in *Current Biography Yearbook 1969* (New York: H. W. Wilson Co., 1969), p. 18.

4. Cortwright, p. 203.

5. Ibid., p. 215.

6. "Apollo 11: First Men on the Moon," *U.S. News & World Report,* July 11, 1994, p. 52.

7. Moritz, p. 20.

Chapter 10

1. Ken Adelman, "Ground Zero," *Washingtonian,* April 30, 1990, p. 67.

2. Ibid.

3. Ibid.

4. Michael L. LaBlanc, ed., *Contemporary Black Biography,* Vol. 1 (Detroit: Gale Research, 1992), p. 197.

5. "Pulled to the Top by His Bootstraps," *Insight,* October 8, 1990, p. 9.

6. Joe Klein, "Can Colin Powell Save America?" *Newsweek,* October 10, 1994, p. 26.

7. Evan Thomas, "Why He Got Out," *Newsweek,* November 20, 1995, p. 45.

8. "Perspectives, " *Newsweek,* November 20, 1995, p. 33.

9. Thomas, p. 45.

Further Reading

Anderson, Marian. *My Lord, What a Morning.* New York: Viking Press, 1956.

Appel, Marty. *Joe DiMaggio.* New York: Chelsea House, 1990.

Cole, Michael D. *Apollo 11: First Moon Landing.* Springfield, N.J.: Enslow Publishers, Inc., 1995.

Gonzales, Doreen. *Cesar Chavez: Leader for Migrant Farm Workers.* Springfield, N.J.: Enslow Publishers, Inc., 1996.

Gould, Alberta. *First Lady of the Senate.* Mt. Desert, Maine: Windswept House Publishers, 1990.

Keller, Helen. *The Story of My Life.* Garden City, N.Y.: Doubleday & Co., 1954, (originally published 1903).

Meighan, Tyrone. "Dr. Hector P. Garcia," *Corpus Christi Caller-Times,* July 3, 1993.

Powell, Colin, with Joseph E. Persico. *My American Journey.* New York: Random House, 1995.

Urquhart, Brian. *Ralph Bunche: An American Life.* New York: W.W. Norton & Company, 1993.

Ziesk, Edra. *Margaret Mead.* New York: Chelsea House, 1990.

Index

Pago Pago, 35
Palestine, 44
Perkins Institution for the
    Blind, 10
Persian Gulf War, 7, 87-88
Philadelphia Choral Society,
    18
Powell, Colin, 6, 83-91
Presidential Medal of
    Freedom, 6, 7, 15, 22,
    31, 39, 47, 55, 63, 71,
    79, 88, 90

Q
quarantine, 79

R
Reagan, Ronald, 63, 86
Reifsnyder, Agnes, 18
Reserve Officer Training
    Corps (ROTC), 83
Roosevelt, Eleanor, 20

S
San Francisco Seals, 50
Saudi Arabia, 88
Scott, David, 76
Shepard, Alan B., 75
Smith, Clyde, 26
Smith, Margaret Chase, 25-31
Story of My Life, The, 13
Sullivan, Anne Mansfield,
    10-15

T
Tau Island, 35
Thompson, Polly, 15
Titov, Gherman, 75
Toscannini, Arturo, 23

Tranquility Base, 73
Truman, Harry, 7
Tutuila Island, 35

U
United Farm Workers
    (UFW), 71
United Nations (UN), 44-45,
    47, 61
United States Commission on
    Civil Rights, 61
United States House of
    Representatives, 25, 26,
    31
United States Senate, 25,
    27-28, 30-31

V
Vietnam, 84-85
"Viva Kennedy," 61

W
Way of Seeing, A, 37
Weinberger, Caspar,
    85, 87
White House Fellow, 85
White, Wallace, 27
Williams, Ted, 52
women, 30-31
World I Live In, The, 15
World Series, 51-52

Y
"Yankee Clipper," 6, 50-51

Z
Zaire, 45, 47

About the Author

Carmen Bredeson, a former high school English teacher, received her master's degree in instructional technology. In addition to fundraising and performing volunteer work for public libraries, Ms. Bredeson now devotes much of her time to writing. Her works for Enslow Publishers, Inc. include: *American Writers of the 20th Century*, *Ross Perot: Billionaire Politician*, and *Ruth Bader Ginsburg: Supreme Court Justice*.